Purpose: copyright © 2017 by Daniel Budzinski

Cover Design: Micaela Frakes-Zieger and Billy Chester
Workbook Design: Micaela Frakes-Zieger

All rights reserved. No portion of this book may be reproduced, stored in a retrieval system, or transmitted in any form or by any means, electronic, mechanical, photocopy, recording, scanning, or other except for brief quotations in critical review or articles without the prior written permission of the publisher or Daniel Budzinski.

Published in Romeo, Michigan by Everest Studios, Inc.

This book may be purchased in bulk for educational, business, organizational, or promotional use.

The quotations do not constitute an express or implied endorsement of Everest Studios, Inc. or any of its content herein by the authors of such quotations.

First Edition

For information, please email support@pioneerpurpose.com

To invite this curriculum into your school, place of worship, business or university, email support@pioneerpurpose.com

Dedication

This book is dedicated to every person looking for purpose, attempting to make an impact in life and seeking to live out their dreams.

Acknowledgements

Elizabeth Budzinski, my wife and partner in life
Everly and Ivy, my two most precious daughters
Karen and Gary Budzinski, my foundation and launching pad
My brothers and sisters who have been my greatest support system
Jesse and Amber Budzinski, for your love, support and belief in the dream on my life.
My mentors and closest friends, you know who you are. I am forever grateful for your love, grace and patience towards me
Jesus, my inspiration, source and hope in life
Billy Chester for his remarkably creative ability and friendship
My entire team that has continued to inspire me by your love and dedication to purpose
Human beings, who will never be satisfied with normality

Table of Contents

Introduction — 4

Section One: Prepare Your Journey — 6

Guide 1: How To Write And Accomplish Life-Changing Goals — 7
Guide 2: The Five Minute Connect — 14
Guide 3: The Inner Competition — 20

Section Two: Evaluate Your Reality And Progress — 40

Guide 4: 33 Ways To Self-Evaluate — 41
Guide 5: Success Vs. Significance — 48
Guide 6: The Best Decision-Making Chart — 54

Section Three: Grow Into Becoming — 58

Guide 7: Learning And Living Your Design — 59
Guide 8: The DreamCycle — 68
Guide 9: Architect Your Vision, Mission And Purpose In Life — 77

Section Four: Sustain Your Impact And Results — 87

Guide 10: Experience Occupational Convergence — 88
Guide 11: Framing Your Life With Your Words, Thoughts And Actions — 96
Guide 12: Building A Culture, Attracting A Community — 103

The Outcome: Book Conclusion — 113

INTRODUCTION

I am currently 26 years old writing this section. As an American, I see and experience reality and life differently than other human beings around the world. My needs, priorities, desires, capacity and problems in life are different from most of the developing world. Yet there is one red thread priority and need that I have found traveling, speaking and listening to thousands of people: **purpose.**

Purpose is at the center of everything. Businesses, schools, universities, governments, religions and even successful families have a distinguished purpose and without it, they fail. Their purpose could be a vision or mission statement, the values they stand for, their plan, target market, goals, or objectives. People are the driving force behind the purposes of these institutions. Individually, people are beginning to understand they have a purpose independent of their company as well.

Each company, school or society has their own purpose too and it should encompass empowering people to access their limitless potential not only as part of the organization but individually also. The greatest companies, schools and societies in the world are those that focus on the purpose of their people. Without people, nothing is possible; yet people are not being equipped for purpose. The absence of purpose-driven activity is the epidemic that companies, schools and societies will have to deal with in this coming age.

The only cure for this widespread disease of a lack of purpose investment in people is to slowly treat the purpose deficiency in individual lives with an antidote. The vaccine that can guard us against the absence of purpose is purposeful activities and lifestyles. That is why I created this book: to serve as an injection to create lives centered around purpose.

I warn you before continuing with this book that when you ring this bell in your life, when you begin to prioritize deep seated dreams, desires and passions, your life will begin to take on new forms. This book was carefully constructed to create change and a shift of pace in your life's progress. Many that have been infected with the disease of a lack of purpose find that their lives are empty and they are meaninglessly existing and barely surviving daily battles, but our plan through this course is to help you become your greatest version, create a life plan, find your purpose deep within and unleash the unlimited potential few have experienced in life.

Purpose: Unlocking Your Limitless Potential

We don't fail by what we do, but by what we don't do.

_____

SECTION 1:

PREPARE Your JOURNEY

✕

So you're on a journey train and it's called life. Everyone's on it and they're not getting off the train for a while. This section is your jumpstart. This section is your preparation for the rest of your life. We will discuss and share topics, ideas and questions that will be thought provoking and challenging. Every journey must have a phase of preparation. Take your time crafting and looking at what you'll need for your future.

We will begin by going through the process of How to Write and Accomplish Life-Changing Goals. You'll then craft your own goals in categories and begin the process of seeing how you can change priorities in your life to line up with long term personal planning.

Next we will have The Five Minute Connect. The single most important and powerful thing in life is relationships. No matter your wealth, social status or possessions, people matter most. No one was intended to live and exist alone. People create the greatest value we can get out of life. Learning how to create a connection, maintain a healthy relationship and reinforce positive and caring emotions towards others is key to growth in our relationships. This experience will be revolutionary if applied.

Lastly we will be going through The Inner Competition. You cannot outperform what you believe. It dictates how you act, think, make decisions and live. It's called your belief system. There are three powerful techniques to help you re-engineer this system: an emotional audit, mind mapping and uncovering rival agreements in existence. Change your beliefs and you'll change your life. Let's jump in.

Guide One

HOW TO WRITE AND ACCOMPLISH LIFE-CHANGING GOALS

Purpose: Unlocking Your Limitless Potential

Goals are the blueprint for a year, the ongoing to-do list for our lives.

Unwritten goals are dreams. Written goals are dreams with deadlines. This guide is designed to help you write out killer goals and increase your ability to see them accomplished. Zig Ziglar said, "A goal properly set is halfway reached." So let's jump in and make dreams a reality.

I am going to share with you three keys on how to write the best goals and increase your success rate of achieving them.

1. CATEGORIES

When you write out your goals start by breaking them into categories. This will help organize your thoughts and build growth measurements in each core area of life.

Great Categories:

1. Mental
2. Physical
3. Relational
4. Financial
5. Spiritual
6. Occupational
7. Family & Spouse
8. Other

No category is more important than the next, but remember the best goals are those you have a passion to accomplish.

Most people ask how many goals they should make in each category. How many is too many? If I create 10 goals for the year and accomplish 100% of them, then I finished 10 goals. If I create 30 goals and accomplish 50% of them then I finished 15 goals.

As long as you don't have the presumption that you're a failure if you don't accomplish every goal, then you're on the right track. Remember, failure is an event, not a person.

2. BE SMART

The foundation for every great goal must filter through the **SMART** acronym. **SMART** means:

Specific — targeting an area for improvement.
Measurable — quantifying the goal.
Assignable — designating the goal to a person.
Realistic — achieving the goal is possible.
Time-related — having a beginning and an end.

———————————

With each goal that you create, ask yourself, "Is it SMART?" Here is an example of a goal that fits perfectly into the SMART criteria—Each month I will put $1,000 towards my mortgage paying off the remaining $12,000 I owe on the loan by year end.

Specific — financial.
Measurable — $1,000/month.
Assignable — assigned to me.
Realistic — it fits within my budget and income.
Time-related — it has a beginning and an end.

Most of the goals created by others are: "lose weight, get better grades, get a job, be more patient," yet these types of goals set you up for failure. There's no plan, no measurability and no way you will be able to measure the success of achieving these types of goals.

SMART goals will help you **target**, **plan** and **achieve** your goals at a new level.

3. MEMORIES

We cannot afford our goals to just center around production outcomes; more importantly they have to produce memories. When our goals only center around performance and exclude people, we will never measure up to what we aspire to and need for ourselves. It's important that our goals produce memories.

Here are a few great questions you should ask yourself before you commit to a goal:

Memory Test

Why am I making this goal? (What's the purpose?)

Does this goal reinforce my priorities and values in life?

Does this goal help create a more healthy lifestyle?

Will this goal promote better relationships?

If your goals don't align with your life and purpose or add value to your relationships, you should probably scrap them. If you answered "no" to any of the questions above, you should scrap that goal. Goals are lifestyles, not life rafts.

Many believe that goals are their life rafts to a better life and future: that a goal can get them where they want to be and help them lead a life worth living. In reality, if the goal doesn't align with how you can live each day, then it's probably not a healthy goal. You can commit to uncommon goals as long as you're willing to live an uncommon life. Just be yourself.

Purpose: Unlocking Your Limitless Potential

CATEGORY	GOALS	DATE CREATED	DATE FINISHED
MENTAL	1. 2. 3. Are they SMART? ☐ Do they pass the Memory Test? ☐		
PHYSICAL	1. 2. 3. Are they SMART? ☐ Do they pass the Memory Test? ☐		
RELATIONAL	1. 2. 3. Are they SMART? ☐ Do they pass the Memory Test? ☐		
FINANCIAL	1. 2. 3. Are they SMART? ☐ Do they pass the Memory Test? ☐		

Purpose: Unlocking Your Limitless Potential

CATEGORY	GOALS	DATE CREATED	DATE FINISHED
SPIRITUAL	1. _____ 2. _____ 3. _____ Are they SMART? ☐ Do they pass the Memory Test? ☐		
OCCUPATIONAL	1. _____ 2. _____ 3. _____ Are they SMART? ☐ Do they pass the Memory Test? ☐		
FAMILY & SPOUSE	1. _____ 2. _____ 3. _____ Are they SMART? ☐ Do they pass the Memory Test? ☐		
OTHER	1. _____ 2. _____ 3. _____ Are they SMART? ☐ Do they pass the Memory Test? ☐		

Writing out your goals is an essential process throughout your life. Some write out 90-day goal lists, some for seasons and others once a year. We suggest that you look at your goals and reflect on them once a week minimally and revise them as an ongoing dream list. Once you've completed this section then move on to The Five Minute Connect where immediately you can see some of your relationship goals and desires come to life.

———

Purpose: Unlocking Your Limitless Potential

Guide Two

THE FIVE MINUTE CONNECT

This exercise is specifically an experience. Our challenge is that you will find three people and do this five minute exercise with them.

Purpose: Unlocking Your Limitless Potential

The purpose of the Five Minute Connect is to create intentional moments where individuals can cultivate and access a new level in relationships. You can use this in your most intimate relationships, to your family, friends, and even strangers. The entire foundation is built on connecting deeper with other individuals and unleashing the power within your mind and life.

3 REMINDERS WHILE CONNECTING

Focus. Turn off all electronics and distractions. Focus on what you're feeling and grasp your thoughts towards the other person as you go through this exercise with them.

Face the person. Put your hands in your lap, or if you're standing, fold them in front of you.

Eye contact. Look into the person's eyes and maintain eye contact. It will create discomfort, but it's actually forming a deeper connection.

Desired Elements for a Connect

What emotions would you like to experience in your relationships?

Honesty	Generosity
Gratitude	Enthusiasm
Forgiveness	Sincerity
Positivity	Appreciation
Creativity	Security
Safety	Valued
Love	Noticed
Peacefulness	Enlightened
Happiness	Heard
Confidence	Considered
Hope	Transparency
Assurance	Compassion
Gentleness	Freedom
Affirmation	Connectedness
Joyfulness	Openness
Humility	Unity
Honor	Trust

When it comes to the five steps on the next page let your answers and statements reflect the principles and emotions above. It's these principles that are the most influential and powerful when it comes to the deep need within all humanity. When we harness these feelings and build upon them it not only opens our minds but our lives to a new level of possibilities.

Purpose: Unlocking Your Limitless Potential

5 Steps on How the Connect Exercise Works
Please read through this entire section before beginning.

―――――――――――――

1. Start a timer for 60 seconds and just look into each other's eyes and simply connect with your eyes. You can smile, laugh, or cry, but let the experience take you somewhere.

2. For 60 seconds you're going to take turns with this statement:

> I appreciate you because...

―――――――――――――

Example:

Intimate Relationships: I appreciate you because you're the most meaningful person in my life.

Work relationships: I appreciate you because you have helped me excel at my gifting and grow in my position.

Stranger Relationships: I appreciate you because there's a sense of trust and warmth in your eyes and person.

―――――――――――――

3. For the next 60 seconds you're going to take turns with this statement:

> One of my favorite things about you is...

4. For the next 60 seconds you're going to take turns saying:

> I forgive myself for...

5. For the next 60 seconds you're going to take turns expressing thankfulness with the statement:

> Thank you for...

Purpose: Unlocking Your Limitless Potential

You can do this once a day with someone that means something to you or create the intentional moment a few times a week, but it's guaranteed to make your relationships healthier and deeper and strengthen your connection with and to them.

This connection exercise can be done in groups, but it's best experienced one on one.

The beauty of the Five Minute Connect is its fluidity. It's not limited to the statements on the previous page, and no matter if it's your first time or hundreth time using it, no experience is the same. The participants can create their own statements and change them up. There are hundreds of other great statements to experiment with. Let's take a look at a few of them.

INTERCHANGEABLE RELATIONAL STATEMENTS

I honor you for...
You make me smile when you...
You're forgiven because...
I trust you because...
Your loyalty makes me feel...
It makes me happy to see you...
One trait about you that I love is...
You're empowered to...
You make me laugh when you...
I appreciate your...
A great trait you carry is...
You are valuable because...
You're loved because you...
I see beauty in you because...
I see your purpose as...
You're worthy of...
When I see you I see...
You're accepted because...
I forgive you for...
The dreams you have in your life are...
I care about your...
You encourage me when...

INTERCHANGEABLE REFLECTION STATEMENTS

I forgive myself for...
I forgive ___ (person in my life) for...
I see myself as... (kind, caring, etc.)
I experience freedom when I...
I am empowered to...
I am valuable because...
My purpose is...
I accept myself because...
I am worthy of...
I am...
I am thankful for...
My deepest desire is...
I am beautiful because...
I have big dreams for my life because...

IT'S KEY WHEN USING THE REFLECTION OR RELATIONAL STATEMENTS NOT TO SPEND A LOT OF TIME THINKING OR SPEAKING. LET IT FLOW AND TAKE TURNS GOING BACK AND FORTH TO GET AS MANY CONNECTION POINTS AS POSSIBLE.

Remember, now that you've read this guide, it's time to put it into action. Don't proceed to the next guide until you've identified three people and asked them if they would do this with you. It could be a classmate, friend, family member, spouse or possibly even someone you just met. After you complete it with those three people, we want you to imagine how you can implement this type of encouragement and connection into your relationships on an ongoing basis.

We now move onto The Inner Competition. This is where you'll audit your emotions, map your mind and look into lies and agreements you've made with limiting beliefs in order to experience transcendent freedom in your life.

Guide Three

THE
INNER
COMPETITION

This guide is one of the longest. I encourage you to take your time and write as much as you can for each answer. Really search deeply and look for what could be limiting you or holding you back in any area or belief system.

Three Incredible Techniques for Inner Engineering

Inner engineering is such a crucial concept when it comes to becoming the person we want or need to be to live out our dream life. Most of us in life have been scripted through our culture, circumstances and lives. We have been taught a set of rules through the norms of society that have limited us from our full potential.

This guide is going to serve you by taking you through the process of taking a look deep below the surface of your heart and mind to find out why you do what you do. We will then go through the process of an emotional audit, mind mapping our subconscious and unconsious mind and our rival agreements. At the end an exercise will help you engage your senses and test your new freedom.

1. EMOTIONAL AUDIT

We usually experience only 12 of our 6,000 emotions that we have words for in the English language. When's the last time you audited your emotions?

Do you often find yourself feeling angry, used, depressed, entitled, sad or mad? Or do you tend to lean on or towards being happy, joyful, excited, motivated, encouraged, pumped, opportunistic and inspired? We have to look at what we tend to emotionally lean and look towards. So what emotions are we empowering in our life?

What we feed on is what controls us. If we feed on negativity, that is what will have power over our mind, will, emotions and heart. If we feed on positivity, it will affect and infect all of our emotions, experiences and encounters. Most of the emotions we tend to lean toward come from deep within us: from our pasts and from our experiences.

What if these emotions were coming from our subconscious and unconscious mind? Let's look a little deeper at this.

2. MIND MAP

The mind operates on three levels at any time: The conscious, the subconscious and the unconscious. It's very important to understand the value of each level and see where your emotions, responses and reactions come from so you can rewire your mind.

Let's take a look at the 3 levels:

THE CONSCIOUS MIND

Your awareness of what's happening around you or inside you.

Example: You're talking, listening, aware of your breathing and the room you're in.

THE SUBCONSCIOUS MIND

Your memory bank of emotions and experiences are your memory recall. The subconscious is the second nature. A repeated behavior that can be done without a conscious thought.

Example: You're talking on the phone and driving while not paying attention yet somehow you remember the directions and get home safely.

THE UNCONSCIOUS MIND

A database of all your unconscious forces, memories, experiences, beliefs, patterns, attitudes and subjective maps that drive behaviors that you've had in a lifetime. They are hidden way below accessibility and must be triggered to become aware of them.

Example: Words are spoken that were said to you, that you buried deeply because of the emotional pain associated to them and you react because of things you're not even concious of.

_____

It is key to understand the levels in our mind and where our behaviors, actions and attitudes are coming from. They are not always in our conscious but are often in our subconscious and unconscious mind. We want to change but we have to be able to understand the situations that have caused us to agree to something that rivals our potential and desires.

Rival agreements are subconsciously and unconsciously operating and stopping us from the changes we deeply desire within our life. These agreements are the invisible forces that move us either forward or backward. Let's take a look at rival agreements.

3. RIVAL AGREEMENTS

Rival agreements are ideas or statements that we've created or fallen victim to from our past or beliefs about our future that compete for our potential and hold us back from changing. They're belief systems limiting and holding us back from reflecting our true nature, desire, personality and potential.

Often, our rival agreements come from fear. Fear of our past, current state, or future. We derive these fears from the experiences of others and our own experiences. Rival agreements are the beliefs under the surface to why we don't do what we need to do. Let's look at a few examples below.

RELATIONAL ISSUES

When you were young you had one relationship end horribly and you promised yourself you would never marry or be emotionally committed to someone. You're older now and wonder why you're not married or have valuable relationships.

BELIEFS ABOUT MONEY

You've heard all your life that "money is the root of all evil," so you made an internal commitment that money is dangerous. Now your relationship to money is unhealthy and you grow up poor, unable to meet your bills or be financially stable. You avoid the talk of money because of the negative connotation you have towards it.

STEREOTYPING

You grew up with a racist father so your stereotype is your competing commitment against a certain ethnic, color or minority group. You go to a school with all minorities and you're unable to connect with others.

FEAR OF FAILURE

Growing up, every time you failed, your parents strictly reprimanded you. Mistakes weren't tolerated and your opinion wasn't validated. Growing up you never shared what you felt with those close to you. You never do anything risky anymore.

THE POWER OF REJECTION

You've personally experienced a friend, lover or family member backstab, betray, break promises or even do unthinkable evils to you. You were rejected. In your life you keep distances in your relationships now and none of them go deep.

FEARING SUCCESS

You've often heard stories of successful people being extreme or eccentric and losing their families. You feel a strong desire and destiny to be significant in life but fear the opinions of others that connect success with broken people. What if success changes my values and heart? What relationships would I lose when I gain money or influence? Consequently, you settle for less and refuse to pursue your greatest potential.

EATING HABITS

You grow up poor and eat once a day. You promise yourself that one day you'll never miss a meal, so when you get older every time you have a hunger pain you snack. Hunger brings back horrific

TIME COMMITMENTS

Long ago you would always wait for others and decided not to be on time. You show up late for everything. You always feel rushed and stressed and don't understand why you can't show up on time. Blaming and creating excuses becomes normal.

PERSONAL PROGRESSION

I want to have better relationships but I'm not willing to take responsibility for my mistakes. Growing up I was the problem for everything, I got blamed for everything and even took responsibility for other people's mistakes. Now I avoid responsibility because it's easier for me to just blame others.

Your rival agreements are identified in frustrations, fears, anger, and negative influences. We all have an abundance of competing commitments working behind the scenes. It's not that we don't want to change, but something underlying in our fears and mind is empowering comfort and safety that competes with our drive to progress.

These evaluations are worthless if you're not honest with yourself. Something will pull you to be politically correct. This isn't for someone else, this is for you. Be raw and real in this next part of the guide and you'll find breakthrough.

Be honest, be open, and this guide will serve you well.

Activity

What is one thing in my life that I'm not doing consistently that I would like to do?

_____
_____
_____
_____

How can I make time, energy and myself available to do this?

_____
_____
_____
_____

Time Commitments

How often do I show up late for things and how can I change that?

_____
_____
_____
_____

Do I find myself blaming others, traffic, time and outside circumstances? What does this reveal?

_____
_____
_____
_____

Do I value other people's commitments and time? If so, yet I show up late, why do my actions contradict my time commitments?

_____
_____

Fearing Success

Do I find myself fearing the future of my occupation or idea in case it blows up and scales?

_____
_____
_____
_____

In what way do I perceive success as a negative? Why?

_____
_____
_____
_____

How often do I experience doing what I love or feel called to as a burden?

_____
_____
_____
_____

How can I change my thinking or actions to align growth and success in a healthy way?

_____
_____
_____
_____

The Power of Rejection

Am I consciously aware of any rejection I have experienced in life that needs to be handled? What do I need to do to deal with this emotionally?

_____
_____
_____

How has rejection affected the way I engage and interact in my relationships?

_____
_____
_____
_____

Has rejection negatively affected my ability to have intimacy with others? How can I find healing in this area?

_____
_____
_____
_____

How can I recognize what has happened and overcome the experiences that are holding me back?

_____
_____
_____
_____

Progression

What would I like to see change in my life in order for me to be more effective and productive?

_____
_____
_____

How am I going to effectuate these changes?

_____
_____
_____

Are there things I desire to do or places I would like to go that I don't because of my inability to continue to evolve and learn? Explain.

___

Eating and Drinking Habits

Do I have a healthy relationship with food? How would I describe that relationship?

___

Does food control my life? (Snacking all day, overeating, etc.) What can I do to have self-control in this area?

___

How would I describe my relationship with alcohol? Is it healthy?

___

What can I do to better align my interaction and relationship to food and alcohol?

___

When did my balance, understanding and interaction become unhealthy with what I eat and drink?

___

What experience is associated with my habits of eating and drinking that creates regret?

___

How can I create new life changes in this area and who can I invite to hear my intentions and help me overcome?

___

Relationships

What is one relationship that is broken that I would like to see healed and whole?

___

Why did this relationship take a downward cycle?

___

Purpose: Unlocking Your Limitless Potential

OUR MOST DIFFICULT SEASONS ARE OUR MOST DEFINING SEASONS

THE INNER COMPETITION

What can I do to help improve and bring restoration to this relationship?

___

Do I find myself talking positively or negatively about people in general?

___

Do I find myself blaming people often? What is my natural response?

___

What can I do to start taking responsibility more often and talking more positively about others?

___

Beliefs

What is one thing I believe or think about myself that is negative that I would like to change? How can I do this?

___

Am I happy with the perception I have about myself? What does that perception look like?

_____
_____
_____
_____

Do I often see and take inventory of my deficiencies and my lack of gifts and talents? Why do I see myself this way?

_____
_____
_____
_____

When I'm disappointed in myself, why am I feeling this way? What can I do to encourage myself?

_____
_____
_____
_____

How can I change my perception and limiting beliefs about myself and my future?

_____
_____
_____
_____

Memory

What memories hold the strongest influence in my life? Are they good or bad? Why?

_____
_____
_____

Purpose: Unlocking Your Limitless Potential

How can I change my mindset about my past and help create a better future for my memories?

_____
_____
_____
_____

Experience

What traumatic experience have I buried and told very few about?

_____
_____
_____
_____

Would sharing this with a close friend or loved one help process through this situation? Why or why not?

_____
_____
_____
_____

How can I go through the process of healing in this area? What could this look like?

_____
_____
_____
_____

Attitude

Is my overall life attitude happy or sad? Why is my attitude this way?

_____
_____

Do I find myself reacting to life more than responding? Who is in control of my attitude? Why?

___

What would my life look like if I decided that my attitude would be positive even in tough times? Is this possible for my life and if so, how?

___

Schedule

Do I find myself complaining about what I've made commitments to in my calendar? Why?

___

Who controls what goes in my calendar? What does this reveal about myself?

___

Do I say yes to calendar commitments because of an obligation to please others? Why or why not?

___

Purpose: Unlocking Your Limitless Potential

What are two things I can require to answer as a boundary to not overcommit myself before I say yes to something entering my calendar? (ex. I don't make calendar decisions without my spouse.)

1. _____
   _____
2. _____
   _____

Behavior

When I don't have accountability, how do I behave with the "rules" in life?

_____
_____
_____

What does this tell me about myself?

_____
_____
_____
_____

Do I see a place for growth in trusting myself and my ability to make positive decisions when no one is looking? What would this look like?

_____
_____
_____
_____

What are two things I can do to take more risk in trusting myself and my behavior?

1. _____
   _____
2. _____
   _____

Spirituality

Do I see myself as spiritual? Why or why not?

_____
_____
_____
_____

Have I ever been burned or hurt by a religious or spiritual person? What happened that stands out?

_____
_____
_____
_____

How has this affected my growth in this area of my life?

_____
_____
_____
_____

Are there things in my life that I can begin to do more of to awaken and revive my spiritual senses? What are they?

_____
_____
_____
_____

How can I surround myself with people more developed in this area and learn from them?

_____
_____
_____

When doing this exercise, it's important to understand that there are no limits to discovering what is competing under the surface to unlock your limitless potential and live out your dreams. This can be filled out weekly to rediscover how to even be honest with yourself.

Now it's time to launch into Section Two, the evaluation of your reality and progress. In this section you'll be looking at self evaluation, a shift in your mindset and your decision making.

———

SECTION 2:

EVALUATE Your REALITY And PROGRESS

You're 25% of the way done. The preparation phase is an incredible beginning to whet your appetite for the possibilities of what your life could look like. We have seen that every journey has milestones where we stop, look back, look ahead and evaluate our current reality. We project our future and evaluate the progress that will be needed to get us there, what needs improvement and the reality of what has been accomplished. We then make adjustments and continue on.

In this section we will start with a self-evaluation guide. It's filled with reflection questions and charts to map out what you're doing great and what could use improvement. Then through engaging questions we will walk you through how to make the adjustments to change your results. This tool helps unlock the limitlessness within you.

Next we go after a common misconception of success. We then replace it with a more accurate and healthy idea of what it could look like in your life. In this day and age significance is success. It's the depiction of scaling your idea, product, passion or business through empowerment rather than greed or gain.

We end this section with a decision-making chart. Feel free to copy this for yourself so that each major decision you have in life you can evaluate your pros and cons and if the what, how and why of the decision line up with your current priorities. Your decisions affect your destiny, so let's begin the section.

Guide Four

33 WAYS TO SELF-EVALUATE

When's the last time you took a careful look at how you live your life?

It's important to reassess to determine whether you're leading the life you've always wanted to live. It's crucial to your success, happiness and future to take an honest inventory of what's true about yourself.

I created this self-evaluation guide so you can assess how your priorities play out and then make the needed changes to get you back on the right path.

Below, read each line and check the box in the section that you most relate to. Next you'll create a plan of action to implement the changes needed to adjust your life onto a better path.

SELF-EVALUATION GUIDE

	The Outcome: Pain Failure Insignificance Emptiness Unhappiness Disappointment	X	The Outcome: Purpose Success Significance Joy Value Fulfillment	X
1	Read as a last resort	☐	Read as often as possible	☐
2	Stopped learning after school	☐	Am always learning	☐
3	Know everything	☐	Am teachable	☐
4	Care about what I can get	☐	Care about what I can give	☐
5	Watch TV and play video games often	☐	Dream big, plan and strategize often	☐
6	Criticize when others succeed	☐	Celebrate when others succeed	☐

Purpose: Unlocking Your Limitless Potential

What evalutaion stands out most above? Why is this highlighted for my life?

___

What evaluation can I most work on above and how? What could this do for me?

___

7	Inconsistent in my choices	☐	Consistent in my choices	☐
8	Have very few life habits	☐	Disciplined in my life habits	☐
9	Let life take me where it wants	☐	Plan out my week	☐
10	Live stingily	☐	Live generously	☐
11	Sleep as often as I can	☐	Limit my sleep schedule	☐
12	No limit on my alcohol consumption	☐	Monitor my alcohol consumption	☐

How can I better plan out my week, choices and disciplines in life?

___

In what way or with what resource can I give more, and who in my life will benefit from that giving and how?

___

13	Need constant supervision to get work done	☐	Work hard without accountability	☐
14	Control others	☐	Empower others	☐
15	Degrade and demean people with my words	☐	Uplift and encourage people with my words	☐
16	Only accountable to myself	☐	Accountable to influences in my life	☐
17	Listen less than I talk	☐	Talk less than I listen	☐
18	Give commands to demand solutions	☐	Ask questions to derive solutions	☐

How can I genuinely care about listening more to people? What benefit will I receive?

_____
_____
_____
_____

When I lead others do I use threats or encouragement? How can I become a better leader and empower others?

_____
_____
_____
_____

19	Can't handle "no" and infringe on boundaries	☐	Can respect "no" and others' boundaries	☐
20	Withdraw or communicate aggressively	☐	Engage or communicate feelings calmly	☐
21	Don't have written goals	☐	Write out goals	☐
22	Ignore personal responsibility	☐	Apologize first and take ownership	☐
23	Lead by what I feel to be true	☐	Lead by what I know to be true	☐
24	Preach what I don't practice	☐	Practice what I preach	☐

Do I have a hard time apologizing and admitting I am wrong? Who is someone that I could ask for forgiveness from today and for what?

_____
_____
_____
_____
_____

Is it difficult for me to handle the boundaries of others? Is this possibly because I have a lack of boundaries in my life? What are two boundaries I can place in my life that can help protect my relationships?

_____
_____
_____
_____
_____

25	Fear change and remove myself	☐	Constantly changing and reinventing myself	☐
26	Money drives my purpose	☐	Meaning drives my purpose	☐
27	Entitled	☐	Grateful	☐
28	Talk about others	☐	Talk about ideas	☐
29	Hold grudges with a long record	☐	Forgive quickly with no record	☐
30	Include who I like and agree with	☐	Include everyone	☐
31	Ignore everyone's opinion	☐	Open to the opinions of others	☐
32	Become bitter	☐	Become better	☐
33	Immobilized by opposition	☐	Motivated by opportunity	☐

Do I find myself talking about people I'm offended or hurt by? Am I willing to approach that person and share my feelings? If not, then what can I do to forgive that person and not allow my experience with them to make me bitter?

_____
_____
_____
_____

Do I only surround myself with people that look, act or think like me? Could this limit my potential and how can I associate with different types of people, minds and achievers?

_____
_____
_____
_____

Do I complain more than I compliment? Why do I act out this way?

_____
_____
_____

PLAN OF ACTION

How can I make adjustments and see the changes I desire in the evaluations above?

1. Can I recognize and see areas of potential improvement in my life? If so where and what can I do to see them improve?

_____
_____

2. If I read this evaluation once a day or week would it make me progress more, become more aware of how to be a better person, or inspire me to become the person I desire to be?

_____
_____

3. Who can I show this evaluation to that I trust and look up to that I can process my thoughts with? What date will I do this by?

_____
_____
_____

4. For the next three months can I look at this guide once a week and watch my life upgrade? What day and time is best each week to do this?

_____
_____
_____

5. What three evaluations above do I believe need the most improvement over the next month that I can focus on to see changes in? What can I do to help move those changes forward?

1. _____
2. _____
3. _____

This guide should be re-evaluated every 2-3 months. You can see your progress, what you've gained ground on and what needs a little more attention. Remember the idea isn't that change must happen overnight or some massive sacrifice has to happen today but just daily purposeful choices in the right direction is how you slowly transform into being the best version of yourself you can be.

The next guide is more of a reflection than an evaluation. Challenge yourself to see something or learn something you never have before. Take some time meditating on a few points that really stand out.

Guide Five

SUCCESS VS. SIGNIFICANCE

Our current ideology of success is money, sex, power. It's being in control, able to buy, do and be whatever you want, being #1, representing the life of the party, and being the center of attention. We pursue this scope of success our entire lives and many get to the end drained and hopeless. Let's take a look at what the difference between success and significance really is.

Today is your day to turn your success into significance, to change your life and never be the same again.

This guide is designed to help you discover the belief system in operation in your life around success and significance, then to help direct your success into significance.

Our culture has become consumed with ourselves. We live in a selfie world and have individually become narcissistic. Narcissism is excessive and erotic interest in ourselves and our physical appearance. We're self-loving, self-admiring, self-absorbed and self-centered and even the best of us should admit that we have fallen into this trap. Our children, families, friends, organizations, dreams and lives deserve better. It will require a higher level of thinking to change our way of living.

True success is important but I'm not sure the word success has what it takes to bring people and families to the other side of their dream in one piece. Success is often defined by your income level, what car you drive, what zip code you live in and your social status. Money can imply a life of success on the surface but it can never give you a life of significance. Because success is what I do for me, significance is what I do for others.

Significance has become a better definition of true success because it's not individualistic, but collective.

Zig Ziglar said it best: "You will get all you want in life, if you help enough other people get what they want in life."

This shift in our thinking is bigger than we can imagine. It has the power to unleash greater passion within you to make a difference and have true success.

Success	**Significance**
is limited.	is unlimited.
dies with you.	dies with who you're building.
the goal: get to the top.	the goal: get others to the top.
is passion.	is compassion.
= making me great.	= making others great.

True success is defined by how many people you make significant.

Please write out your first response to the questions below:

1. Do I think through the lens of success or significance? In what way?

___
___
___

2. How can I live more intentionally to see others succeed around me?

___
___
___

3. Do I put my time, money, energy and focus into what makes me great or others great? How?

___
___
___

Purpose: Unlocking Your Limitless Potential

SUCCESS IS LIMITED. SIGNIFICANCE IS UNLIMITED.

SUCCESS VS. SIGNIFICANCE

4. When is the last time I added value to someone else's life and what did I do?

_____
_____
_____

5. Do I help others succeed in life or am I just worried about myself? How and why?

_____
_____
_____

6. What can I do for someone that would add significance to their life? Who is it that I can do this for?

_____
_____
_____

7. How can I change my direction and focus away from a success thought life and towards a significance thought life?

_____
_____
_____

8. What are three things I can do for others to help them succeed that I don't normally do and that would place me out of my comfort zone?

_____
_____
_____

9. How often do I think about money/posessions versus how often I think about meaning/people?

_____
_____
_____

10. Am I things-centered or people-centered? Does my life revolve around what I have or who I help? How can I take more time and invest in others?

___

Don't reach the top and hate the view.

Remember that money doesn't bring you success—people do. We really don't need more people, organizations, entrepreneurs, millionaires and celebrities promoting a brand of success that's full of empty aspirations and shallow relationships that ultimately leave people empty and broken!

If you want to be successful, understand how to be significant in the lives of people around you. If you want to make it big, give enough people around you what they want. You will find that all your needs will be met in the process.

We need more people of significance, people that have paid the price few have paid: the price to be the greatest versions of themselves.

I am confident that deep within all humanity is a desire for significance. To be known by what we're given and not by what we've gained. To be etched into history by the acts of kindness and goodness we've shown others. History might be stories told about you in books distributed to education systems, stories told by your family and friends to others, or the impression and love you gave to those around you. In this next guide we will take a better look at what it takes to make great decisions that align with your current priorities in life.

Guide Six

THE BEST DECISION-MAKING CHART

To truly live is to live with no regrets. This guide is going to transform your thinking process to decision-making and prioritization of those decisions with your current needs and purpose in life. During this exercise think of a decision you're currently facing. Here you will process out the value in doing it or not.

Purpose: Unlocking Your Limitless Potential

So many people live with regrets because of their decisions.

What if you could make great choices? What if you could live without regrets?

What if our decisions gave us greater purpose and brought us closer to living out our dreams?

 Every day **35,000** decisions are made per person.

 90% of people say they have a major regret in life.

 $15,762 is the average household credit card debt.

 75% of purchases are impulse buys.

 1 in 4 homeowners have buyer's remorse.

 $27,141 is the average auto loan debt per household.

 31% of people regret their tattoo.

 Only **27%** of college grads have a job closely related to their major.

 $48,172 is the average student loan debt per household.

 50% of marriages end in divorce.

 80% of people dissatisfied with their jobs don't quit.

I want to take you through a decision-making chart to help you make great decisions. This guide is all about how to prioritize your life and decisions.

Answer each question below before you make a decision.

If your answer for why doesn't add up to your priorities and purpose in life, then don't do it.

For every decision you make, ask yourself: what, how and why?

		Pros	Cons
1	What am I going to do?		
2	How am I going to do it?		
3	Does this line up with my priorities?		
4	Does this add value to my purpose?		
5	Why do I want to do this?		
6	Should I really do it?		

Making good decisions is simply a byproduct of knowing what you want and see in your future and making sure your choices will bring you there. Leading the life of your dreams is as simple as **1 + 2 = 3**.

1 is knowing your future.
2 is making sure all your decisions are next steps to that future.
3 is your future outcome.

Section three is going to be incredible. We will be looking into the cycle it takes to accomplish a dream, learning and understanding your design and passions, and architecting some of the most valuable components of your life.

———

SECTION 3:

GROW Into BECOMING

✕

There are seasons to prepare and seasons to reflect and evaluate that lead to seasons of focus and growth. In this section you will be stretched to think big. It might be overwhelming to come up with ideas, answers or thoughts for the questions but allow yourself time to reflect and expand your current idea of reality.

First we will be looking into one of the most key components of life. It's getting a better understanding of yourself. Your passions, dreams, identity, desires, gifting and talents are all a vital part of you learning your design in life. You were born to be different and it's time to expose it.

Next we will jump into the DreamCycle. The process of dreaming, creating, innovating and persisting your dream. Too many dream only at night, soon to wake up to the harsh reality of their lives. You were meant to live bigger than you dream, so get ready to expand your potential!

Then we go onto one of our favorite guides—Architect Your Vision, Mission and Purpose in Life. When you understand your guiding image, value and feeling, you will be an unstoppable force to fulfilling your destiny. Few dare to become all they were meant to be, but those that dare will one day become.

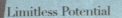

Guide Seven

LIVING AND LEARNING YOUR DESIGN

When I say the word design what comes to mind?

Everything designed has a function. It has beauty and it's been created with intelligence and uniqueness to provide a solution for others. The best designs are simplistic yet internally complex. They serve a purpose and have intentional utility.

A lightbulb transfers electrical energy into light energy. An electrical current runs through a one-inch coiled piece of tungsten between a positive and negative terminal. When reaching temperatures over 4,532° F it begins to emit light. The power is immediate. The inert gas within the glass regulates the temperature and captures electrons to keep the filament from overheating.

The amount of testing, ideation, design and perfection that went into creating the bulb we have today is incredible. Individuals continue to make it better, brighter, and longer lasting. It serves a function that allows us to drive in the dark, watch movies, light our homes and has hundreds of other functions we benefit from.

Limitless Potential

When you know your design you express your destiny.

What if you could learn your design? What if encapsulated in your design was a life filled with joy, purpose and passion?

You are distinct. You have intelligence to create. You have a sound, a thought and an idea that no one else has. You're simplistic yet complex in nature, your personality and desires are looking to express your design.

Often graveyards are full of **unlived dreams, uncreated ideas, unstarted businesses,** and **untaken risks.**

Let's take the journey to discover your path to fulfill your design.

1. Design: Who

Who am I? Identity. I am...

Design isn't what you do—it's who you are.

If someone were to ask you, "who are you?" you would most likely reply with what you do, where you work, your occupational associations, labels, degrees or accomplishments.

When you strip away your labels and activities, what are you left with? It usually starts with **I am…** I am entrepreneurial, I am giving, I am passionate about business and sales, etc.

Whyology. Why I exist. Purpose.

Design goes deeper than "what;" it answers why. Why you exist. Why you're doing what you're doing. Why you wake up, why you sacrifice, why you work hard. If we don't understand our why we will fall short of reaching higher and accomplishing big things.

Design is the thing we give no effort to, we just are.

Knowing our purpose and whyology is essential. It's like having a lightbulb but never placing it in your lamp and turning on the switch. If you don't know its purpose it won't be used to its highest potential.

Purpose: Unlocking Your Limitless Potential

Gifting. Desire. Passion.

Design is what you could do every day without getting paid to do it. It's your passion project. It's that deep desire you don't share with everyone. It's what keeps you up late and keeps you grinding early. It's what you feel you were born to do.

The convergence of our design is discovered in the intersection of our passions, purposes, desires and dreams.

There's no formula to finding your design. There isn't one way. All roads lead to its convergence. Follow these paths and you will see more clearly each day.

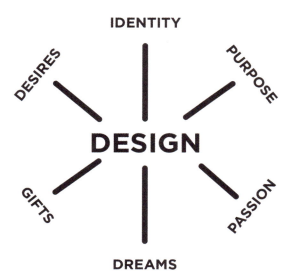

62

Great questions to ask yourself while uncovering your design:

Who am I? (Start with I am...)

I am... _____

I am... _____

I am... _____

I am... _____

Why do I exist? What is my purpose?

_____

_____

_____

_____

What do I burn for and what sets my drive?

_____

_____

_____

_____

What gifting and innate passions do I have in life?

_____

_____

_____

_____

If I were dropped onto the planet with no grid, no financial, physical, mental or spiritual limitations, where would I live and what would I do?

_____

_____

_____

2. Strategy: How

How I do what I do
How I excel at what I do
How I differentiate what I do
How I can do it better than others

Strategy is so key and important after you begin to clearly see your design. Strategy is all about planning, building and differentiating.

Differentiation: How I excel in my idea industry

The human mind only notices and sees what's different.

Don't be like everyone else; that's boring.

Let's say you build printers. How can you do this in a way that differentiates you from everyone else? How can you design it uniquely, create new technologies, keep it efficient and cost effective for others?

If you provide a service, how can you create a culture that provides the most humble and incredible human service and customer experience? How can you add your unique angle to your industry?

Strategy isn't where you rush to "doing," it's where you plan culture, values, and excellence and build out how your product, business or activity is actually going to excel.

Great questions to answer while building your strategy:

Do I often skip to action and activity before strategizing on how I can be different? Why?

_____
_____
_____
_____

When is the last time I reflected on creating a different outcome in my life, relationships, ideas or businesses? What changed?

_____
_____
_____
_____

Am I just reacting to everything around me and my competitors or do I feel like I am executing a strategy that will get me to my outcome or goal? How can I see a greater outcome?

_____
_____
_____
_____

What can I do to differentiate my life, business or idea?

_____
_____
_____

How can I do what I do utilizing my gifts and abilities? What is my unique drive to be better?

_____
_____
_____

3. Activity: What

What I do
What I give my attention to
What I give my resources to

Activity is what we rush to first, later realizing we have no passion for what we do or no strategy to execute a plan to scale our idea.

Design + Strategy = Opportunity
Activity ≠ Opportunity

Opportunity can spread us thin and make us ineffective, missing out on our design.

We rush to action, quickly give our attention to things that don't line up with what we want to do or who we are. We give our resources to things quickly, to then soon regret all our prior decisions.

When it comes to activity it best flows first through design and strategy.

Great questions to answer before rushing to action or opportunity:

What can I do that best represents my design and strategy?

_____
_____

Do I find myself chasing opportunity, stressed or anxiety driven by my activities or actions? How can I change my approach and mindset when it comes to design?

_____
_____

Am I giving my resources to things that do not align with my design? (Time, money, energy and relationships.)

_____
_____

Purpose: Unlocking Your Limitless Potential

How can I better steward my resources and attention so that I can be more effective in my purpose?

_____
_____
_____
_____

What can I sell, provide or create that would generate great value for others?

_____
_____
_____
_____

What can I give or do that would make others' lives or businesses better?

_____
_____
_____
_____

What solution can I offer that would meet someone's need?

_____
_____
_____
_____

Understanding your identity is the most important part of design. I always remind myself that everything worthwhile takes time. Everything great didn't happen overnight. The process of a baby being born takes nine months of growing pains. When you begin this process, we encourage that you take time to think throughout your day and reflect on ideas and who you are and want to be in life. This is a source for many things yet to come. Let's continue to move forward.

Guide Eight

THE

DREAMCYCLE

If you ask someone "what is your dream," most will reply with a long lost and forgotten idea of the past or a strong desire they feel will never come true. Accomplishing a dream is a process. It's not a mystical or mysterious process only awarded to the chosen or few, it's given to the dedicated and committed. Get ready to dream big.

The process of upcycling is taking an old item and reusing the materials to create something better.

This concept works in all areas of our life. It's a never-ending cycle of producing something greater from the remains of an old dream or idea.

Whether it's a better marriage, product, friendship, idea, culture, society, world or solution, every idea or dream must process through this cycle to progression.

What if you could dream big? What if you could live bigger? You were meant to live bigger than your dreams. So let's go through the practical steps to accomplishing your dreams. I call it **the DreamCycle.**

PHASE 1: DREAM

Every great idea starts with a dream or idea; everyone has one, but few go to Phase 2 and create it. If you've never dreamed then you've never lived. It's the feeling of capture and escape. It's the feeling of suspension as you look through the eyes of your destiny at yourself and see your limitless potential.

What's your idea or dream? Close your eyes and imagine your life limitless: if you weren't constrained by anything financial, geographical, relational, physical or mental, then what would you do? What would your relationships look like, your future, your occupation, your free time? Where would you choose to live?

WRITE WHAT YOU ENVISION BELOW.

_____
_____
_____
_____
_____
_____
_____
_____

THINGS TO CONSIDER IN THIS PHASE:

1. First and most importantly, are you or can you get passionate and excited about your idea? Why or why not?

Purpose: Unlocking Your Limitless Potential

THE BEST DREAMS HAPPEN WHEN WE'RE AWAKE

THE DREAMCYCLE

2. Who are a few trusted friends or people in your idea industry that you can get feedback from about the direction of your future and idea? Write their names and 2–3 questions you'd ask them.

_____
_____
_____
_____

3. Can the dream/idea be something others can get excited about too? Why do you think so?

_____
_____
_____
_____

PHASE 2: CREATE

Creating dreams is invigorating, it's empowering, it's addicting and it surges through you as you make an unknown variable known. An unknown possibility seen, an idea a reality, a dream a lifestyle. Yet it's the most difficult phase considering the time, energy, focus, confidence and execution it will require.

GREAT PREPARATION QUESTIONS:

1. What are you willing to put down or give up in order to create your dream?

_____
_____
_____

2. What amount of resources can you create in the next 6–12 months to commit to producing your dream life? Develop a plan for each resource commodity below.

Resource Commodities:

1. Time: Write out the time frames for each week and day you will dedicate for the next 6–12 months towards the building of your dream/idea. (ex. Tuesdays 7–10 pm, Thursdays 6–8 am)

_____
_____
_____

2. Money: What amount of money can you save in the next 6–12 months to spend on the dream/idea? Write out a plan to save these funds.

_____
_____
_____

3: Influence: What relationships in your life are strategic for your idea category or industry that will help connect the right people to this dream? How can you build a better relationship with them? How can you build influence in your idea industry? How can you stretch your influence capacity during the next 6–12 months?

_____
_____
_____

4. Expertise: What can you do to enhance and grow your expertise in your idea industry in the next 6–12 months? Are there books, videos or resources that you can consume and grow your expertise in during this time and if so what are they?

_____
_____
_____

PHASE 3: INNOVATE

Every dream that's created must innovate or it will die. Innovation is a continuum, it's the ever-evolving purpose of what you envisioned years ago but will possibly require decades to perfect. This phase can be done before or after Phase 2 (or both) but it's paramount for the growth and development of your idea.

WHILE INNOVATING ASK YOURSELF:

1. What can I improve about my idea?

_____
_____
_____

2. Is my idea brand new to the world, building on what's been done, or innovating a current model, idea or product?

_____
_____
_____

3. Does my dream, idea or product make other people's lives better and is it about benefitting me or about benefitting others?

_____
_____
_____

4. Who can I invite that I trust to give me feedback on what I'm doing? Write their name(s) and call them for feedback. Write 2–3 questions for them to challenge your idea on.

_____
_____
_____

5. How can I improve my strategy on making my dream/idea accessible to others?

_____
_____
_____

6. Can this idea scale or is it bottlenecked because it can't be automated?

_____
_____
_____

PHASE 4: PERSIST

This is the most important phase. All must persist and overcome obstacles. Dreams can take a lifetime: so don't create unsustainable or unhealthy living to see your dream become a reality overnight. During this phase we will look at all possible adversities and barriers to dissect our idea. We must push through the grind of logistics, plans, implementation, tactics, marketing, creation, innovation and find ourselves going back through the DreamCycle.

This phase is all about the grind.

It's where you're getting your idea out. You're promoting it, selling it, fixing it, packaging it and more.

Companies and pioneers that didn't persist in reinventing their dream into its reinvention go bankrupt, not adapting to new technologies, cultural trends, ideas and flow. Never stop persisting to find yourself back at the drawing board discovering a better way and usefulness for your idea. I want to give you a few keys necessary in this phase.

4 KEYS TO BUILDING SUSTAINABILITY:

1. Set up your goal.

2. Break it down into manageable increments.

3. Put someone in charge.

4. Monitor the process and the person.

After you've spent time in this phase, you will cycle back to Phase 1—and since you've finished your first trek, now it's time to start Trek 2 and dream again with your idea(s).

What part of the DreamCycle are you in and what's the next step? This exercise is intended to help reinvent the dream and grow it. There is no end to the possibilities, only the ones you create. There's no limit to a dream, only the one you set. So never stop dreaming, creating, innovating and persisting. The day you do is the day your dream dies with you.

Know that the DreamCycle isn't just about ideas, products or businesses. It also can relate to your relationships, peronal development or growth. Reflect and use it where purpose is needed most.

Now we'll begin to transfer into building out your vision, mission and purpose in life. These aspects are guiding forces to be reckoned with. When we know our vision we no longer live like victims and our mission moves us into momentum. Those that don't know their purpose will only recreate their past. Your future is as bright as you make it.

Purpose: Unlocking Your Limitless Potential

Guide Nine

ARCHITECT YOUR VISION, MISSION AND PURPOSE IN LIFE

Purpose: Unlocking Your Limitless Potential

IN THIS GUIDE YOU'LL DEFINE YOUR:

Vision as a guiding image
Mission as a guiding value
Purpose as a guiding feeling

Can you imagine driving a car with your eyes closed and expecting to arrive at your destination? What about building a thousand-piece puzzle without seeing the cover photo? How about constructing a massive building without any architectural plans? It's just not possible.

No one plans on failing in life — yet when we fail to plan, we plan to fail. We plan our vacations, meetings, grocery lists, college paths and weekends; yet, not many plan out their families or future.

If you're climbing a mountain how would you prepare? To ensure your safety and chance of accomplishment, you'd envision the summit, map the trek, and inspire the journey. You'd define each day of travel, how much food and water would be required and what gear you'd need to complete your journey.

Having the end in mind will help dictate the path, preparation and decisions in your journey.

Defining your vision, mission and purpose is paramount to reaching the top and enjoying the view. We're all climbing the mountain of life and expecting to get to the top. So let's break down the key elements to your road map to the future.

1. ENVISION THE SUMMIT

Vision pictures summiting the mountain and overlooking the world. Envision yourself at the top of the summit. You've arrived. Finding the desire to start is difficult, but envisioning the summit will energize you. Everything made is created twice. Once in your mind when you envisioned it and once experienced in reality.

Envision your future. Visualize the best possible outcome and set your sight on achieving it. Vision empowers you to dream outside of reality and into the unseen realm of possibility.

Everything seen was once unseen.

Your internal vision drives your external reality. What image is leading your life right now?

Can you envision your future? Is it bright, positive and full of life? What specific images do you see for your life when your eyes are closed?

_____
_____
_____

Are you able to dream bigger than just surviving and providing for today's needs? If not, what's holding you back? If so, what does this look like?

_____
_____
_____

If nothing changes in ten years, where will you be and what will you be doing? Are you fully satisfied with that image? If not, what changes can be made in your internal vision to create a future that will totally satisfy your heart's calling?

_____
_____
_____

three peaks of society you feel the greatest desire to lead in.

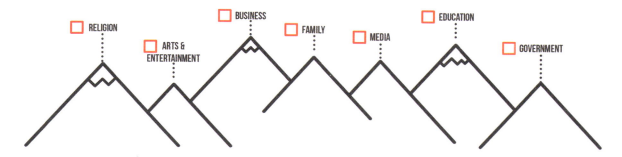

When you envision the future, where would you like to see your life, family and occupation? Define images of accomplishment or arrival in these areas.

Personal life: _____
_____
_____

Family: _____
_____
_____

Occupation: _____
_____
_____

If you could live, do, build, and be whatever you wanted to,

What would you do? _____
_____
_____

What would you build? _____
_____
_____

Where would you live? _____
_____
_____

Who would you be? _____
_____
_____

What three visions for your life represent the most energizing picture of you summiting mountains of achievement in the future?

1. _____
_____

2. _____
_____

3. _____
_____

Out of the three visions, which is most important to you? Why is it most important and how can you prioritize this in your life?

_____
_____
_____

2. MAP THE TREK

Your mission is the map of daily values and principles you stick to while trekking up the mountain. Then your values will help define the culture for those that choose to join you.

I like to break mission into three categories that keep you focused on achieving your vision and goal:

> **Values**
> **Principles**
> **Culture**

Values

Values are the truths you believe based on morals given to you by family, society, culture, experiences and your inner voice. They are custom to you and only a personal experience can help you to question or compromise your current values.

CIRCLE THE 10 VALUES THAT MEAN THE MOST TO YOU AND NUMBER THEM.

How can you implement practicing these values daily? Can you commit to reading your top 10 values once a day?

_____
_____
_____
_____
_____
_____
_____
_____
_____

FAITH	LOVE
GROWTH	PASSION
SIGNIFICANCE	INCLUSION
SUCCESS	JUSTICE
EXCELLENCE	FLEXIBILITY
INTEGRITY	OPEN-MINDEDNESS
RESPECT	SUSTAINABILITY
TRANSPARENCY	HARMONY
CREATIVITY	GIVING
STEWARDSHIP	LEADERSHIP
EMPOWERMENT	FUN
HOPE	FREEDOM
HONOR	POSITIVITY
HONESTY	COMPASSION
ACCOUNTABILITY	SIMPLICITY
COMMITMENT	EQUALITY
TRUST	HELPING
INNOVATION	HUMILITY

Values can be taught positively or negatively. Experience largely affects our value system. For example, let's say you've been cheated on. You pick up a value of distrust. Ultimately, it can take a lot of positive experiences with others to help restore your value of trust from a powerful experience of distrust.

Principles

Principles are global fundamental truths that transcend personal and societal experience or knowledge. They are universal realities that affect and guide humanity forward. When principles are followed, you will experience transformation in your life.

During the journey you will need principles that assist your decision making and automate your ability to stay focused on your vision.

What are six life principles you can commit to that best represent who you are and uphold your personality and character? (ex. Treat others with respect, no matter the circumstance.)

1. _____
2. _____
3. _____
4. _____
5. _____
6. _____

Culture

Culture is the collection of chosen values used to guide and protect the focus of your group. It's the values and principles you stand for that others can attach themselves to. People can then commit to your tribe, business or family guided by strong values and principles to success.

What are the five most important values in your life that can be solidified in the culture for your life, family & business?

What type(s) of people do you desire to attract in your culture? (ex. positive, joyful, encouraging)

1. _____
_____

2. _____
_____

3. _____
_____

4. _____
_____

5. _____
_____

- _____
- _____
- _____
- _____
- _____
- _____
- _____
- _____
- _____

It's important to evaluate who you want to attract since you will only maintain attraction with those of like values. Your culture sets the tone for who can run with you. Everything has a culture. If you don't set the culture, someone else will.

3. INSPIRE THE JOURNEY

Purpose is the guiding emotion that propels you forward when your body, mind and others say stop. Purpose is the meaning of why you're traveling the road you're on. **Purpose gives sacrifice a meaning.** You're not on the journey because of your vision, values, principles or culture. All of this came because you first had a uiding emotion, a purpose that was making you dig deeper and look far on the scope of the horizon and see the possibilities of a brighter future.

No one climbs Mount Everest because they can. They do it because the cost of not doing it becomes greater than the possibility of death attempting the summit. That all-consuming feeling inside pushes them to do the unthinkable. They feel it's their destiny to summit, their only hope for happiness and ultimately their duty and passion in life, so they climb. They have a vision because they first knew their purpose.

Since sacrifice finds meaning in purpose, what are you willing to give up to go up in life?

Your purpose is grafted into your identity. It's the "who am I" statements. Strip away your labels, profession, degrees and associations, and what are you left with? I am passionate... I am entrepreneurial. Your purpose helps you discover your underlying passion and drive.

I am... _____   **I am...** _____

I am... _____   **I am...** _____

I am... _____   **I am...** _____

Your vision is the ability of visualizing the peak of success in your life. Your mission is the values, principles and culture that guide you through your vision. Your purpose is what keeps you out late and gets you up early. It's the sanity to your insanity. When you architect the full picture of your future then you can accomplish whatever you set your heart to.

Doesn't it feel refreshing and inspiring to know that you can reach the top by simply discovering and defining your purpose? The joy must be in the journey. The only fight to win is the one within your heart and head. Your vision, mission and purpose will evolve and we encourage you to write up these vision, mission and purpose statements and revise them often. Also, make sure to read them as often as you can a constant reminder of where you're headed. Now it's time for our final section.

———

SECTION 4:

SUSTAIN Your IMPACT And RESULTS

We prepare, we evaluate, we grow and then we sustain. Once we sustain our healthy current state we can then start the process over. We can continue to expand our capacity, understanding and destiny by building on what we've accomplished and done in the past. This phase is all about using process and values to harness the sustaining power of transformation.

First we will look into what it takes to experience occupational convergence. It's taking what you love and merging it with what you're gifted at, while getting paid to do it. There is a special calling on your life, and you deserve to live it out. You'll go through types of jobs, types of people, types of problems, the four pillars of focus, and the four axioms of success.

Next we audit your words, thoughts and actions. Actions are the keys to deeper activities taking place. So many want to hijack their living but they can't without these tips. When you go through this guide, you'll understand human behaviors at another level. You'll see others in a new light and begin to bend the reality and possibility on your life. Sustaining impact is all about maintaining the ground you've won and taken. This guide is all about understanding what it takes to maintain your new mindset and belief systems of limitless living.

We believe that becoming the greatest version of yourself is largely about being surrounded by people with this similar desire. You are what you read, listen to and watch and most of that involves other people. We will end your entire experience by talking about culture and how to learn, live and lead that culture. Whether it be your family, friends or community, this will be a core element to growth and sustenance.

Guide Ten

EXPERIENCE OCCUPATIONAL CONVERGENCE

While you're reading through this guide take moments to ponder and think honestly about your life and your current occupation. Being honest with yourself is key to leaving this exercise equipped with the knowledge of what type of person you are and what type of person you must become to experience convergence. This doesn't happen overnight though, so enjoy the process.

In this guide, you'll discover convergence from your occupation into your destiny.

In life, people commit to one of three functions of work:

1. A job

2. A career

3. A calling

Which one do you have and which one do you want? How can you bridge the gap to get the one you want?

_____
_____
_____
_____
_____
_____

We commit to work a job, career or calling because of the motivators in life:

1. What I can get paid to do

2. What I'm gifted and talented to do

3. What I love and have a passion to do

Occupational convergence happens when you find the intersection of all three of these motivators in your occupation and life.

Circle which motivator singlehandedly dictates your choice and type of work commitment.

Ultimately, we get what we want. If we don't want much we won't have much. Many are working for "the man," and they're dissatisfied with their job and life. Others go through life wishing they could have someone else's life or type of work.

People get what they want out of life. It boils down to the three different types of people in the world:

1. People who wonder what happened

2. People who watch what happens

3. People who make it happen

Purpose: Unlocking Your Limitless Potential

Circle which person you feel best represents you.

Do you find yourself wondering why everything bad happens to you in your life and why you can't get ahead? Then you're someone who will go through life continuing to wonder what's happening. Are you more of a bystander in life, watching life pass you by, or are you the one that no matter what, you're jumping in, making things happen and moving life forward?

Remember: you choose, you commit, and you decide what will motivate your life.

People who make things happen understand that they are the solution to their problems in life.

Purpose: Unlocking Your Limitless Potential

WHEN YOU WORK YOUR PASSION, YOU'LL NEVER WORK A DAY IN YOUR LIFE.

EXPERIENCING OCCUPATIONAL CONVERGENCE

This helps you to know who you should spend your time with, be close to, learn from, aspire to be like, and ultimately who you choose to be.

This now traces to the types of problems we face each day. I call them the Three Prescripted Problems.

1. Problems I create

2. Problems other people create

3. Problems the ecosystem creates

If you're driving and you hit someone's car, then you created the problem. If someone else is driving and they smash into you, then they created the problem. If you're driving and a tree falls on your car, then the ecosystem created the problem.

It doesn't matter who created it or what caused it; in the end, only you can be the solution to your problem. When we stop blaming others, the world, or the system for the issues we have in life, we will begin to experience a more virtuous life.

What significant problems do you have in your life that you can be a solution for?

___

___

___

Do you find yourself blaming others or the ecosystem for the life you've been given? (circle one) Why?

YES **NO**

___

___

___

What are three actions you can do daily to change that mindset?

1. _____
2. _____
3. _____

Ultimately our ability to hone into our calling and live in occupational convergence starts and ends with what we focus on. If you're dissatisfied with the results of your life, then you need to change your focus, because what you focus on will produce change and results.

THE FOUR PILLARS OF FOCUS

① What you focus on you'll find.

If you're looking for the bad, you'll always find it in others.

② What you focus on will grow.

Your problems are only fixed by focusing on your solution.

③ What you focus on shapes your reality.

Your reality isn't reality. Your focus is.

④ What you focus on you'll become.

You take on the form of the person that you focus on.

If your life was a tree and you were producing bananas but you hated them, would you be allowed to blame the sun, soil, owner or type of water? No! The fruit is produced as an external reality of what type of tree it is.

If you don't like the fruit on your tree, then you need to plant a new tree.

Are you seeing the results you want to in life?

YES **NO**

Give two ideas on how you can change your focus to attain more of the results you desire in your life.

1. _____
   _____
2. _____
   _____

If you look into the mirror and don't like what you see, you don't have an option to change the mirror. You can only change what you see in the mirror, which is you.

We all then want to create success. Below is the simple formula to success creation.

THE FOUR AXIOMS OF SUCCESS

1. Create virtuous values 80% of your results come from 20% of your efforts. Put your effort into virtuous principles and values and results will come.

2. Make thoughtful decisions Focus on what you're good at and become great at it—then become the best at it. Don't just focus on what you're not good at.

3. Live with considerate intentions Your intentions are summed up in selflessness or selfishness. What intentions drive your actions and how can you change that?

4. Choose authentic actions Act on the things that reinforce your values, decisions, priorities, principles and lifestyle.

Change your focus and your reality will shift. Become the person you want to be. Success isn't making perfect decisions, it's having the right intentions. You control your problems, and only you can control you. It's as easy as making the choice to become the greatest version of yourself today.

Commit to occupational convergence in your life. Be a person that makes it happen and remember that you're the solution to any problem you face.

Now, we'll focus in on the power of our words, thoughts and beliefs and how they control and dictate our actions. It's the mind hack to sustaining change.

———

Guide Eleven

FRAMING YOUR LIFE WITH YOUR WORDS, THOUGHTS AND ACTIONS

They say, "sticks and stones will break my bones, but words will never hurt me." But is it true? In this guide we'll expose the power behind the words and thoughts that dictate your actions.

If I were to put you into an MRI scanner—a huge, donut-shaped magnet that can take a video of the neural changes happening in your brain—and flash the word "NO" for you to read for less than one second, you'd see a sudden release of dozens of stress-producing hormones and neurotransmitters. These chemicals immediately interrupt the normal functioning of your brain, impairing logic, reason, language processing and communication.

What you speak is what you think, what you think is what you believe, and what you believe is what you will take action on.

Words create thoughts, and thoughts create words. They both reinforce each other.

Let's try an exercise. Don't think or imagine a pink elephant. If I started to talk about a pink elephant and asked you not to think about a pink elephant, what would you be thinking and seeing? The pink elephant. Why? Because it's impossible to not see or think about what you speak because our words shape our thoughts.

You believe what you think and you think what you believe—ultimately becoming what you think and say. Your belief system sets the tone for what you'll become. Have you ever audited your words and thoughts to discover their power in operation of your life?

WORDS = THOUGHTS = BELIEFS = ACTIONS

If you want to change your actions, change your beliefs. If you want to change your beliefs, change your thoughts. If you want to change your thoughts, change your words.

Purpose: Unlocking Your Limitless Potential

You will always imitate what you imagine.

When the words and thoughts within you resonate an image for your life, you begin to move in the direction of that dominant image. You become what you behold.

You cannot look at the pink elephant and not think about it. They are one and the same, therefore what you see also will dictate the thoughts and the direction of your life.

We desire a change in life and attempt to change our actions—but soon after, we return to our old selves because our words, thoughts and beliefs haven't changed.

What you believe dictates how you behave.

You will create what you say and think about all day long.

Your visible world is created through your invisible world.

You can't blame anyone for the responsibility of your thoughts.

Your thoughts dictate what you think to be true, not always what is true.

"We can't solve our problems with the same level of thinking that created them." –Albert Einstein

98

Purpose: Unlocking Your Limitless Potential

Let's take a look a few layers deeper within us to create the life we desire around us.

Write 10 statements you can say to yourself every morning that line up with who you are and where you want to go.

1. _____
2. _____
3. _____
4. _____
5. _____
6. _____
7. _____
8. _____
9. _____
10. _____

Write 6 statements you've said to yourself that have held you back or hurt you, and commit to never think of them again. (This is only for you to be aware of the words that you've given power to.)

1. _____
2. _____
3. _____
4. _____
5. _____
6. _____

Right now, repeat this out loud: I am a…

DREAMER
STARTER
ENTREPRENEUR
PIONEER
ACHIEVER
LEADER
TRAILBLAZER
DESIGNER
BUILDER
FORERUNNER
VISIONARY
CHAMPION

DOER
IGNITER
INNOVATOR
INVENTOR
RISK-TAKER
CREATOR
TRENDSETTER
MASTERMIND
PACESETTER
GENERATOR
EXPLORER
MOTIVATOR

How did that feel?

Say these phrases out loud:

I WILL OVERCOME AND PERSIST.

I WILL WIN AND NOT LET DOWN.

I WILL NOT GIVE UP OR GIVE IN.

I WILL OVERCOME EVERY TRIAL.

I WILL WORK SMARTER AND HARDER.

I WILL LIVE MY LIFE WITH PURPOSE.

I WILL FINISH WHAT I START.

I WILL DO WHAT FEW HAVE DONE.

I WILL GET TO WHERE FEW GO.

I WILL HAVE AN AMAZING DAY.

I WILL EXCEL AND THRIVE.

I WILL BE GENEROUS AND JOYFUL.

WHAT IF YOU COULD READ THIS AT THE START OF EVERY DAY? What effect do you believe it would have on you?

_____
_____
_____
_____
_____

We often think and talk about ourselves better than we actually are, which is why we have a hard time with feedback and becoming a better version of ourselves.

When you're critiqued or criticized by others, how do you react and what do you think? Do you ignore or discredit what's said, or justify yourself, or do you investigate, ponder or initiate more conversations to hear how others experience you?

_____
_____
_____

Do your words reflect a lack or an abundance mentality? Lack is "I have to," abundance is "I want to" or "I get to." What are statements that empower your responsibility to have an abundance mentality?

_____
_____
_____

Do you complain about others more than you celebrate them? Why is that?

_____
_____
_____

RATE YOURSELF:
1 BEING THE LEAST AND 10 THE GREATEST, CIRCLE A NUMBER BELOW

How much of your wording is positive?	How happy are you with the way you think and talk?	How strong is your ability to receive criticism or feedback?	How often do you speak reinforcing words out loud?
1 2 3 4 5 6 7 8 9 10	1 2 3 4 5 6 7 8 9 10	1 2 3 4 5 6 7 8 9 10	1 2 3 4 5 6 7 8 9 10

Are your words about life, yourself and others more positive or negative? Why?

_____
_____

Purpose: Unlocking Your Limitless Potential

Do you find yourself talking and thinking negative things about others, or about the good in those you see?

_____
_____
_____
_____

How can you begin to speak and think more positively about your situation, life, and others?

_____
_____
_____
_____

Do you believe your life is where it is now because of what you've thought and said? If so, are you happy with where your words and thoughts have brought you? If not, how can you change that?

_____
_____
_____
_____

Remember—your words are the foundation for a healthy lifestyle. If you want to change your actions, start by shaping your beliefs and thoughts with powerful, life-giving words.

It's time to end your experience with a bang. Building a culture will be invigorating, encouraging, and essential to building a community you can do life with while you trek up your journey.

Guide Twelve

BUILDING A CULTURE, ATTRACTING A COMMUNITY

Mark Twain said, "The secret to getting ahead is getting started." You're already ahead because you just started.

Building a culture is paramount to growing and sustaining a vision. It's important to have a vision for your future, friends, family and finances. It's equally important to have an established culture because culture sets the tone to arrive at that vision in a healthy way.

Cultures are blueprints for visions. Vision is the destination, culture is the expedition. You would never start building a structure without a blueprint—so why do we expect to fulfill a vision without a cultural blueprint?

Our relationships, organizations, families and countries all have a culture. Ultimately, everything has a culture.

Let's take a look at three important factors when building a culture.

CULTURE

Culture is the attitude, behavior, and core values understood and shared by a group of people.

Cultures form in two ways:

1. Through the process of time, creating themselves.
2. Through the process of a leader, created intentionally.

If you're not intentional about creating your culture, your culture will create itself.

BE the culture you intend people to BECOME.

BECOME the culture you want to BUILD.

We can strongly influence and lead people down the roads we have traveled in life.

LOVE the culture you desire to LEARN.

LEARN the culture you desire to LIVE.

LIVE the culture you desire to LEAD.

Leaders love, learn, live, then lead the culture they want to grow. Loving is in your heart, learning is in your head, living is in your actions, and leading is in the influence connection you have in others' hearts by how you live.

Have you allowed your culture to be led by you or others? Have you created your culture or has culture created you? What can you do to better lead your personal culture?

Do you love, learn and live the culture you're a part of? If not, why? If so, what can you do to better represent its values?

_____
_____
_____

Have you committed yourself to living a healthy culture? How do you practically do that?

_____
_____
_____

CULTIVATION

Cultivation is the process of preparing land for crops. Laborers pull out the old trees, thick grass and rocks, and plow the land to prepare for the new seeds that will produce fruit.

Culture is the ground we choose to cultivate our values, gifts, and life. In Alaska, it's impossible to grow corn on glaciers, but in Mississippi the ground has been cultivated and the environment, temperature and surroundings create the perfect place to cultivate healthy crops. In an unhealthy culture, it's impossible to grow healthy people. We must cultivate a positive environment and relational atmosphere where people can grow and excel.

Then, cultivate the culture within. Cultivation is the process of fostering, promoting and developing the growth of something or someone.

Cultivating people and culture is long-term thinking and leadership. Conforming people to culture is short-term thinking and leadership.

Building a healthy team, community, marriage, family, and culture takes longer, but the return pays huge dividends in life.

Purpose: Unlocking Your Limitless Potential

WHEN YOU LEAD, SUCCESS IS CONTINUALLY GROWING YOURSELF WHILE GROWING OTHERS.

BUILDING A CULTURE, ATTRACTING A COMMUNITY

Do you create a healthy environment for people to become the greatest versions of themselves, or do you make it difficult for others to excel? How can you better create a safe place in your culture?

_____
_____
_____

Do you think long term or short term when it comes to building others and what you're doing? Are your activities transactional or transformational? How could you build with longer term results in mind?

_____
_____
_____

Are there any aspects that could make your environment in your business, home, family, etc. more peaceful and healthy?

_____
_____
_____

What are some unhealthy values or actions in your culture that need to change?

_____
_____
_____

COMMUNITY

Community is a feeling of fellowship with others as a result of sharing common attitudes, goals, interests and identity while practicing common ownership.

Community is the byproduct of a healthy culture. People will gather and come if they have a culture that attracts them.

Does your community rally around a person or principles and purpose? Why or why not?

_____
_____
_____

Do you have documented and written common attitudes and values that individuals can recognize as a part of their personal core values in life? How often do you talk about them?

_____
_____
_____

How do you allow others to practice common ownership in your culture?

_____
_____
_____

Cultural core values become antidotes to poisoned, negative, or unhealthy cultures.

Let's check out a few incredible cultural values.

Obsessive About Purpose

This is NOT my job. This is my choice, my passion, and my life. Most people just want to check in and check out. Most people wake up thinking, "Do I have to go to work?" or "I don't want responsibility nor do I desire to excel because I am not fulfilling my purpose."

Mark Twain said, "The two most important days in your life are the day you are born and the day you find out why."

Do you help people find purpose in what they're doing to build your vision? How do you accomplish that?

_____
_____
_____

How often do you help people that work with you discover the purpose of their lives?

_____
_____

Demanding Positivity

No matter what's asked of us or what we have to accomplish, we don't focus on what can't be done but how can it be done. We don't act on or complain about what we're not good at, but develop new skills every day. We remove words like this from our minds:

I don't know how to do that...
I can't do that...
I'm not good at that...

Our problem is our attitude, not the issue itself. We crave finding new ways to solve old problems.

Honor is Key

It's more difficult to honor the people you know, do life with and work with than those outside of your circle. Honor has everything to do with communication. The way we respond, react, and act in situations with each other.

Situations don't shape our honor. Our honor shapes situations. Only you are responsible for how you honor others.

Honor produces environments where people are powerful and own their self-control. Honor empowers people to manage their love, honor, communication, freedom and life through self-control.

Honor creates judgment-free zones allowing people to take risks and make mistakes without the fear of being mistreated, neglected or punished for a failure or mistake.

Is your leadership setting the tone for negativity to be bred through the culture? How can you create a more positive environment?

_____
_____
_____

Do individuals use phrases like the ones on the left? How can you change the way they think about problems to shift mindsets more towards solutions?

_____
_____
_____

Does your communication and confrontation have honor at the forefront? What phrases reinforce honor in confrontation?

_____
_____
_____

Is your environment free for people to take chances and not be rejected for failure? How can you make your environments more free?

_____
_____
_____
_____
_____
_____

Empowerment is Rare

Empowerment flows both ways, from top to bottom and bottom to top. Everyone is looking for permission to move and lead. Too often, leadership is seen as disempowering individuals. People are brilliant, and it's our job to guide them while empowering them to create, be, and produce the best they can.

Is your culture all about empowering others to take action? How can you better create this?

_____
_____
_____
_____
_____

I Have Ownership

We aren't shareholders looking for a quick boost in stock price, we're owners, completely invested in the future of this culture. Why? Because our work is a part of our purpose. Owners don't have a job description per se. They prioritize their time based on the skills they have and what no one else can do to continue to move a vision forward. People love information and leaving them in the dark is the worst way to create ownership.

Do you allow your team and people that love you to be privy to the information you're processing or ideas for the vision or do you only share it with a select group?

_____
_____
_____
_____
_____
_____

Always Looking to Vision

Am I outwardly driven by my needs, or driven to change a world because I'm focused on solutions? We run a culture of vision, not a culture of need. Needs don't move us, vision does.

When you're always trying to meet a need, you will always be in need. Vision sees solutions, needs see problems. The needs of others cannot control my choices but my vision does. My vision sets the priorities of my life.

Are you constantly going from one need to another? Are you driven by vision or need? Why?

_____
_____

Are you focused enough to where your vision dictates your time, energy, people, resources and money? If not, how can you build boundaries around your vision so that you can stay focused and accomplish it?

_____
_____

Teamwork First

African Proverb—if you want to go fast go alone, if you want to go far go together.

Teamwork is the accelerated promotion of your successors. We celebrate the successes of people beyond us, beside us, and behind us. We create an "I win you win" mentality and culture.

Your legacy will only carry you as far as you commit yourself to carry others. We can only transfer in our legacy what we championed in our lives. A slave can't teach freedom to a slave, only a free man can teach a slave freedom. We carry each other across the finish line.

Do you leave people in the dust or do you take the time to develop them to be equipped for their positions? How do you do this?

_____
_____
_____

How often do you create opportunities to celebrate the promotions, successes and wins of others?

_____
_____
_____

Do you treat people like employees working for "the man" or team members accomplishing a bigger purpose?

_____
_____
_____

What would your life look like if you could live out these values and make them cultural norms?

_____
_____
_____

Out of the cultural values above, what three stand out to you the most and why?

1. _____
2. _____
3. _____

You were born to create culture. To lead people through the values that govern healthy habits and lifestyles. Be and build your culture today.

THE OUTCOME

Take a deep breath. It's just the beginning. Massive changes, big sacrifices and monumental shifts are not the true signs of transformation. Small, daily and progressive choices are the full picture of your life taking on its best form. I am honored that you have completed this book. You are part of a community that values meaning over money, purpose over profits, people over promotion, and ultimately your potential over your problems.

You've done it. You said yes to your greatest version and finished. I encourage you to share your answers in this book with someone you trust. Begin to surround yourself with people further along and better than you. Begin to make daily choices that reinforce your larger vision in life. By completing this book and putting in effort, you just took a massive step in the right direction.

If you're looking for more ongoing development, curriculum or help please visit DanielBudzinski.com or visit my social media pages and let's connect. I publish podcasts, videos and blogs weekly to inspire this purposeful culture we intend to build and be a part of.

Lastly, now that you've finished this course, please email me and let me know so I can personally congratulate you:
support@pioneerpurpose.com

Always remember that your dreams are worth living, you're worth investing in, and you have incomprehensible value. Until next time, keep pioneering.